A Pinch of S

'Nose, nose, jolly red nose,
And who gave thee this jolly red nose?
Nutmegs and ginger, cinnamon and cloves,
And they gave me this jolly red nose.'

Beaumont & Fletcher,
The Knight of the Burning Pestle

Also by Desmond Briggs
Entertaining Single-Handed (Penguin Books)

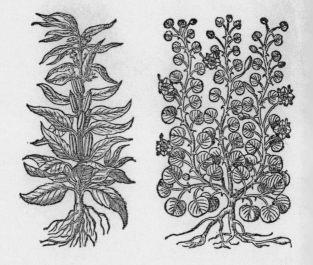

A Pinch of Spices

Picked by Desmond Briggs

Blond & Briggs

For ICD

Illustrations from
The Herball or Generall History of Plants
by John Gerard, 1597
Commentaries on the Six Books of Dioscorides
by Pierandrea Mattioli, 1563
Handbook of Plant and Floral Ornament
by Richard G. Hatton, 1909

Cover illustration:
Hindu perfumer mixing spices
from *The Book of Perfumes*,
Eugene Rimmel, London 1865

First published in Great Britain 1978
by Blond & Briggs Ltd, London
and Tiptree, Colchester, Essex
Designed by Humphrey Stone and
Printed in Great Britain by
The Compton Press Ltd, The Old Brewery
Tisbury, Salisbury
in Linotype Granjon
on Design Cartridge
© copyright 1978 Desmond Briggs

ISBN 0 85634 087 1

The Storage of Spices

All spices should be stored in airtight tins, in a cool dark place. If they are exposed to the air, they will lose their savour; and sunlight bleaches out their colour and their strength. Racks of pretty bottles with gay labels may look attractive but should be shunned by the spice-picker. Most spices keep well in the whole form (*i.e.* unground); cloves and pepper in particular have a name for longevity, but this depends on their being protected from the air.

The Use of Spices

Ideally, we should grind the small amount of each spice as and when we need it, just as we do with pepper. This may not be practicable, and it makes sense to grind an ounce or two at a time, and store it in an airtight tin until your culinary whimsy calls for it. Label the tin, of course, both for identity and for sudden inspiration when you are composing a stew. Be very ginger with the use of spice, especially when you are not following a recipe. Never exceed the stated dose in a recipe; you would be surprised how some spices, overused, can dominate and ruin a delicate dish.

The Grinding of Spices

Ideally, you should use a pestle and mortar, but the mechanically equipped may resort to an electric coffee-grinder kept for spices only: grind to a powder, run through a fine sieve and store in an airtight tin.

The Toasting of Spices

Some spices, such as coriander, cumin, fenugreek and poppy seed, should be lightly toasted before grinding. Use an iron frying pan for this.

The Spices

Allspice

Pimenta Officinalis
Jamaica Pepper
Pimento
France: toute-épice
Italy: pepe di Giamaica
India: kabab cheene

Allspice is an evergreen tree, 40–100 feet tall, growing in Jamaica, Mexico, Guatemala and Honduras. The allspice berries are the dried fruits, picked when still unripe. It is the only major spice which comes from the Western Hemisphere alone, and it takes its name from its flavour, which is said to be a combination of cloves, nutmeg and cinnamon

The Maya Indians used allspice to embalm their dead.

Francisco Hernandez, who was exploring in Mexico for Philip of Spain, first came upon the allspice tree and named it *piper tabasco*, for he found it in the Tabasco region. It is still a secret ingredient of that famous hot sauce

We use allspice, whole in pickling spice, marinades and sometimes when boiling inexpensive fish; a few berries sprinkled in green pea soup (as the Dutch do) add a spicy flavour. We grind allspice for use in curry powders, some cakes and Christmas pudding

Anise

Pimpinella Anisum
Aniseed
France: anis
Italy: anice
India: suara

Anise is an annual, native to the Middle East.
Its distinctive liquorice flavour has been used for
thousands of years

The Romans used anise in their sweet-wine cakes
(see Cato: *De Agricultura*); they recognized its
value as a digestive and for checking wind. In 1305,
Edward I placed a tax upon it, which suggests that
it was a habitual import; and according to the Royal
Wardrobe Accounts of 1480, the Royal under-
clothes were scented with little bags of 'fustian
stuffed with ireos and anneys'

Anise is much used in the distinctive spirits and
cordials of the Mediterranean; the French have
Pernod and Anisette, the Greeks Ouzo, the Turks
Raki and the Arabs Arrack

The scent of anise has a wonderful attraction for
dogs, and it is much used in drag-hunting and in
the famous hound trails of Cumberland. It also
features in many pet foods

We use the seed in cakes, and a few leaves may be
tossed into a salad

Caper

Capparis Spinosa
France: câpre
Italy: cappero

Capers are the unopened flower-buds of a trailing
shrub belonging to the Mediterranean, which
resembles in habit the common bramble. The plant
is cultivated in Sicily and the South of France

Capers are appraised according to the time when
the buds are gathered and pickled. The finest are
the tender young buds called 'non-pareil', after
which, increasing in size but lessening in value,
come 'superfine', 'fine', 'capucin' and 'capot'

The Ancient Greek physician, Dioscorides, prescribed the roots and leaves of the caper bush for
easing swellings

Capers are always pickled in wine vinegar and
thus sold; do not let them dry out. Their sweet
yet astringent flavour is due to capric acid which
only appears when they are pickled

We use capers in sauces and as a garnish. In
England, boiled mutton with caper sauce is as
traditional as boiled beef and carrots. They are
also used for Sauce Tartare, and may be added to
salads and stews

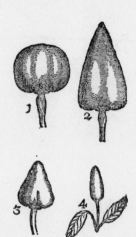

Capsicum

Capsicum Annuum
India: Buri Murch

Cayenne pepper, chillis and paprika all come from
the Capsicum family (see under separate headings)
as do red pepper, bird pepper, bell pepper and green
'peppercorns'. The Capsicum is a member of the
nightshade family of plants, like the potato and the
tomato, and is no relation of true pepper. The con-
fusion arose because the Spaniards went to the New
World expecting to find in those Indies the rare
and expensive oriental black pepper. Before the
Spaniards arrived, the Maya Indians used them
medicinally, calling them *ic*: onomatopoeiacally,
they were good for nausea, cramp and diarrhoea

In 1493, Columbus had brought back to Europe
'peppers more pungent than those from Caucasus'
and their cultivation soon spread to most warm
climates. The Capsicums are a vigorous enlivener
of many tropical dishes and add a welcome variety
to the monotony of subsistence diets

Bell, or sweet peppers, may be used green or ripe.
Raw, they add a crunchy difference to salads; they
may be stuffed and baked; used as a colourful
garnish; and they feature in such classical dishes
as Chicken à la King

Caraway

Carum Carvi
France: carvi
Italy: comino
Germany: Kümmel

Caraway seeds come from a hardy perennial herb with feathery foliage like carrots. It is an ancient spice; traces have been found in Neolithic lake dwellings, Isaiah commended its cultivation, Shakespeare referred to it in *Henry IV*, Part 2, when Shallow says – 'Nay, you shall see my orchard; where, in an arbour, we will eat a last year's pippin of mine own graffing, with a dish of caraways' – and Prince Albert is said to have reintroduced it to England

The Germans used to place a platter of caraway beside a child's cradle to drive away witches. The Greeks recommended oil of caraway as a tonic for pale girls.

Caraway seeds may be chewed to sweeten the breath and avert belching.

Kümmel, the Dutch and German liqueur, tastes strongly of caraway
We use caraway in rye bread, in soups and stews of a Teutonic bent. The young leaves may be chopped over a salad and even the roots, when boiled, make an interesting vegetable

Cardamom

Elletaria Cardamomum
France: cardamome
Italy: cardamomo
India: Elachi

An important and pungent oriental spice, cardamom seeds come from a perennial shrub growing high up in the Cardamom Hills above the Malabar coast of India. The ancient Egyptians chewed the seeds to keep their teeth white; in India in the fourth century B.C. they were prescribed to reduce fatness; and when the famous Minoan Linear-B tablets were deciphered by Michael Ventris twenty years ago and they were found to be invoices from one merchant to another, cardamom featured prominently

Apicius, the Roman Robert Carrier, recommended the use of cardamom in his recipe for *Oxygarum*, *To Promote The Digestion*

The Arabs use cardamom seeds in their coffee; they believe that it cools the body, soothes the stomach and acts as a powerful aphrodisiac. The Indians chew the seeds

Oil of cardamom is an ingredient used in the perfumeries of Grasse and in some eaux-de-cologne

We use cardamom in curry powders and in pastries, baked apples and fruit salads

Cayenne

Capsicum Frutescens
Guinea Pepper
Spanish Pepper
France: cayenne/poivre rouge
Italy: pepe di Caienna

Cayenne pepper is ground from small hot capsicums, varying in colour from red to orange to
yellow. The heat lies in the seed and the pod and
can vary enormously, even in capsicums from the
same picking. They grow mainly in Japan, India,
Thailand, Turkey and Mexico, though not in
Cayenne, from which town in Latin American
Guiana their name comes

Medically, cayenne has been deployed against gout
and scarlet fever; taken in large quantities, it acts
as an irritant poison

The taste of cayenne is impaired by damp or by
exposure to sunlight

Cayenne should be used with restraint, for its
biting flavour can overwhelm the palate. It is an
excellent garnish: a light dusting of its bright red
powder can transform a dull dish or a too-bland
sauce. It spikes a barbecue sauce and marches well
with the handsome lobster in Sauce Newburg

Celery Seed

Apium Graveolens
Smallage
France: céleri
Italy: sedano

Celery seed is the dried fruit of a wild plant of the parsley family, native to southern Europe. This wild celery, also known as Smallage, is not the same as the familiar vegetable; the seeds are small and brown; the pungent taste is tenacious

Traces of wild celery in the form of garlands have been found in Egyptian tombs of the twentieth dynasty. The Romans used celery seed as a garnish, and Apicius advocates its use in a sauce for sucking pig

Celery salt is a combination of ground celery seeds and fine salt, much used as a condiment and delicious when sprinkled over tomato juice

Celery seed is used on bread and rolls, in prawn cocktails and fish dishes, in stews and soups, pickles and chutneys – an all-round, much loved spice

Chilli

Capsicum Frutescens
Birdseye peppers
Devil peppers
France: piment enragé
Italy: peperone
India: chota mirch

Chillis are small, fiery capsicums, red and orange.
The Aztecs used to mix them with herbs and other
spices to make a condiment and today *chilli powder*,
a blend of ground chillis, garlic, oregano, cumin
and other spices is used in the Mexican 'Chili con
Carne'

When handling fresh chillis, it is wise to wear
gloves, for they are so hot they may burn the skin.
In Swahili, it is called 'pili-pili ho ho' which is
what you will say if you use too much of it

If you infuse a chilli for two or three months in a
well-stoppered bottle of vodka, you will produce a
fiery spirit which will make your Bloody Marys
truly sanguinary

Whole chillis are used to flavour pickles and vinegar. Chilli powder goes into some spaghetti sauces,
Boston Baked Beans, and many Mexican dishes
like their Guacamole – avocado pears mashed with
onion, tomato, oregano, a little olive oil and salt

Cinnamon

Cinnamomum Zeylanicum
France: cannelle
Italy: cannella
India: Dalchini

Cinnamon is a glossy evergreen bush native to
Sri Lanka and the spice we know is the bark,
peeled off, dried and tied into short bundles of
quills like cheroots. Cinnamon and its sister-spice
Cassia, which comes from China and Sumatra,
are perhaps the oldest spices known to man, for
in Chapter XXX of *Exodus*, God commended
them to Moses as an ingredient of anointing oil.
The Talmud gives an exact recipe –
'Balm, onycha (or cloves), galbanum, frankincense,
of each seventy manehs; myrrh, cassia, spikenard,
saffron, of each sixteen mannehs; costus twelve;
aromatic bark (cassia lignea) three; cinnamon nine;
soap of Carsina, nine kabs, Add wine of Cyprus. . . .
If one mixed honey with it, he made it unfit for
sacred use; whilst he who omitted any one of the
ingredients was liable to the penalty of death.'
This would probably be considered an over-severe
penalty for careless cooks today, but serves as a
warning that we do well to be precise in the use
of spices

Cinnamon has been used in the East for many
centuries in the Temples, to mask the unwhole-
some smell of the flesh in burnt offerings

Nero buried his wife with a year's supply of cinnamon, and a Frankish monastery in A.D. 716 ordered five pounds of it to be sent to Normandy

In the seventeenth century, when the Dutch took Ceylon from the Portuguese, they imposed a strict monopoly on the cinnamon trade which the British East India Company assumed in 1796 and hung on to until 1833

Cinnamon used to be prescribed to calm down mothers during a rough childbirth. It is good for coughs and colds, expels wind, and is astringent

Cinnamon is bought ground or in sticks. Ground, it has a stronger flavour, but should be stored in airtight glass jars

We use whole cinnamon sticks to spike hot drinks, punches and mulled wines. It can be added to boiling mutton or ham. Ground cinnamon is sprinkled over junkets, rice puddings and custards; it adds a new dimension to stuffed cabbage or grilled pork chops; and hot, buttery cinnamon toast on a winter's day after a long walk is a heart-warming survivor from the traditional English nursery

Cloves

Syzygium Aromaticum
(Eugenia carophyllata)
France: clou de girofle
Italy: chiodi di garofino
India: loang

The clove is the nail-shaped flower-bud of a variety
of myrtle tree; the name comes from the Latin
Clavus and the French *clou*, both meaning nail.
The buds are picked when they are pale red and
dried in the sun until they turn dark brown. The
clove tree is native to the Spice Islands (Moluccas),
but nowadays the longest and best cloves come
from Zanzibar and Penang

In the Han dynasty in China (fourth century B.C.)
cloves are referred to as 'chicken-tongue spice'. By
Roman times, they were being imported through
Alexandria, and they soon became one of the most
prized and expensive spices; the household records
of the Countess of Leicester in 1265 note that
she paid ten shillings per pound. The Portuguese
annexed the Spice Islands and the lucrative trade
in 1514; in 1605 they were expelled by the Dutch,
who imposed a complete monopoly in the six-
teenth and seventeenth centuries. In 1770 the
French managed to smuggle some clove seedlings
to Mauritius; by 1818, they were also established in
Zanzibar and the Dutch monopoly was shattered

In the Spice Islands, the Moluccans used to plant a clove tree for each child: this provided a kind of birthday book for the child, and if the tree failed, the child was doomed

Oil of cloves has for centuries been effective against toothache

A pomander is an orange stuck with cloves: this exudes a delicious aroma for months. They used to be carried by men of dignity in the presence of malodorous persons; nowadays they can be used in place of artificial deodorants in bathrooms and lavatories and as a sweet moth repellant

In the kitchen, we use cloves for bread sauce, for studding hams, in marinades and mulled wines, and frequently with cooked apples

Coriander

Coriandrum Sativum
France: coriandre
Italy: coriandolo
India: dhania

The coriander plant is an annual of the parsley family. The leaves give off a pungent stink (hence the name, from the Greek *Koris*: a bedbug), but the dried ripe fruits have a flavour said to resemble honey and orange peel

The ancient Egyptians used it for medicine and for spicing, and it was one of the provisions laid on by Jehovah for the Israelites – (*Exodus* 16:31)

Coriander was recommended in *The Thousand and One Nights* as an aphrodisiac, and in the Middle Ages too it was used as a love potion

Today, coriander comes mainly from Egypt, Mexico and Bangladesh

Coriander seeds should be lightly toasted before grinding. Make sure the seeds are ripe: unripe coriander has an unpleasant taste. They are a most important part of many curry powders, and are used in stuffings for poultry, in baking, with pork and for sprinkling on milk or fruit puddings. The parsley-like leaves may be pounded to a paste and used with ginger in a mild curry

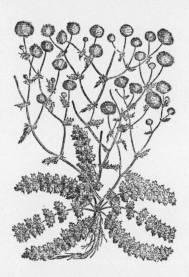

Cumin

Cuminum Cyminum
France: cumin
Italy: comino
India: jeera

Cumin is a small plant of the parsley family. The seeds are actually the dried fruits. The plant is grown commercially in India, China, Indonesia, Japan, Iran, Turkey and Morocco

In the Gospel according to St Matthew (xxiii 23), we find Jesus reprimanding the Pharisees for taxing spices diligently – 'for ye pay tithe of mint and anise and cummin' – while neglecting more fundamental necessities like faith and charity

From Pliny we learn that the ancients took the ground seed medically and that it was accounted a good remedy for squeamishness. It was also found to occasion a desirable pallor of the face (Horace: *exsangue cuminum*)

Cumin seeds help the digestion and in India they provide a little bowl of them, lightly toasted, to be nibbled during the course of dinner

Cumin is a most important ingredient in most curry powders. Both the Dutch and the Germans flavour cheese with it, and it figures in many Mexican national dishes

Curry Powder

France: curry
Italy: curry

Curry powder is not, of course, a spice itself; but,
as a blend of many different spices, it has its place
in many spice cupboards and in this book. The
word comes from the Tamil *kari*, to eat, and curry
is the traditional staple of Indian cooking and a
main ingredient of many oriental dishes

The *Indian Domestic Economy and Receipt Book*,
published in Madras in 1850, lists the following
ingredients of curry – 'Anise, coriander, cumin,
mustard and poppy seeds; allspice, almonds,
asafoetida, butter or ghee, cardamoms, chillis,
cinnamon, cloves, cocoa-nut and coconut milk
and oil, curds, fenugreek, nuts, garlic and onions,
ginger, lime juice, vinegar, the leaves of *Bergera
Koenigii* (the curry-leaf tree), mace, mangoes, nutmeg, pepper, saffron, salt, tamarinds and turmeric.'
Hardly something to knock up in a spare five
minutes, possibly, but it is rewarding to prepare
your own, as does the Indian housewife

Here is a standard recipe from Rosemary Hume, using ingredients that are easily obtainable –

- 2 tablespoonfuls each of turmeric, cumin and coriander
- 1 tablespoonful each of powdered ginger and cinnamon
- 2 teaspoons each of fenugreek, chillis, cardamom and mace
- 1 teaspoon each of mustard, cloves and poppy seed

Grind what needs to be ground, mix all together, sieve and store in airtight containers in a cool place. Curry powder actually improves with time as each spice blends in with the rest

Hotness is not an essential feature of curry. It is interesting to note that the hottest ingredient – chillis – originated in Mexico, and only arrived in the East some time after the Spanish Conquest. The Chinese and the Indonesians favour milder curries, and the power of a curry powder can easily be adjusted by diminishing the quantity of the hotter spices

Fennel Seed

Foeniculum Vulgare
France: fenouil
Italy: finochio
India: soanf

Fennel is a well-known perennial – to the Anglo-Saxons it was one of the nine sacred herbs – and the seeds are harvested when they are hard and grey. Its properties have been valued through successive civilizations; Culpeper noted that – 'the seed, if it be boiled in wine and drunk, is good for those who have been bitten by a serpent, or have eaten poisonous herbs'

Fennel seeds infused in water provide an effective eye lotion. It may be added to a baby's gripe water, and is good for earache, toothache and coughs

Fennel seeds have a flavour reminiscent of anise, but less dominant. They are used in bread and cakes, on top of rolls and fruit tarts, and may be added to some curry powders

Fenugreek

Trigonella Foenum Graecum
Goat's Horn
Greek Hay-Seed
France: fenugrec
Italy: fieno greco
India: methi

Fenugreek is an erect annual of the bean family.
The seeds are contained in a pod shaped like a
goat's horn. It has long been grown around the
Mediterranean, in North Africa and India. It has
a bitter taste, like burnt sugar

The ancient Egyptians used it for food and to
diminish fevers. It also figured in their rites of
fumigation and embalming. The Greeks and
Romans cultivated it as cattle fodder

Fenugreek has been used medically for stomach
ailments and an ointment made from it helps
mouth ulcers and chapped lips

Fenugreek is an ingredient of Halva, and is often
used in curry powders and chutneys

Ginger

Zingiber Officinale
France: gigembre
Italy: zenzero
India: adrak

Ginger is the rhizome or underground stem of a tall, reed-like tropical plant. The best comes from Jamaica; Chinese ginger is mild

It is mentioned by Confucius, by the Greeks, and in the *Koran*. It was an important staple in commerce between Europe and the East, and appears in duties levied at Acre in 1173, Barcelona in 1221, Marseilles in 1228 and Paris in 1296

Ginger is sold dried, whole, or ground. It is also crystallised and preserved in syrup. Fresh ginger can be found, and is excellent in curries, mashed to a paste

Ground ginger may be used in baking, in chutneys and pickles and curries. It is delicious with pork. Do not forget gingerbread, which was a favourite sweetmeat of Elizabeth I

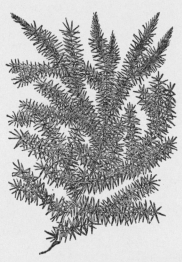

Juniper

Juniperis Communis
France: genévrier
Italy: ginepro

Juniper is an evergreen shrub, growing in temperate climates. The berries have a resinous flavour and are used in the distillation of gin (which word comes from the French *genévrier*). In England in the seventeenth century, they were thrown on the fire in the sickroom to fumigate and sweeten the air. Culpeper commends them thoroughly – 'They provoke urine exceedingly; they are also good for a cough, shortness of breath, consumption, pains in the belly, ruptures, cramps, and convulsions; they strengthen the brain, help the memory, fortify the sight by strengthening the optic nerves, and give safe and speedy delivery to women in labour; they are excellent good in all sorts of agues, they help the gout and sciatica, and strengthen all the limbs of the body'. Surely a handy sort of spice

A few berries make an excellent addition to stews, and with game they complement the high flavour. If they are crushed with a wooden spoon and stuffed inside a roasting bird, they add a rare and special piquancy

Liquorice

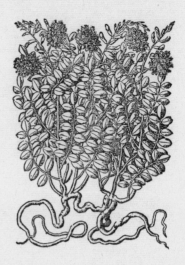

Glycyrrhiza Glabra
France: réglisse
Italy: liquirizia

These hard black sticks are the rendered-down juice of a hardy perennial. To the sweet taste of the root the plant owes its generic name, of which liquorice is a corruption. The plant came originally from the East and came to England in the Middle Ages, when it was popular as a cure for coughs

In the monastery at Pontefract in Yorkshire, they cultivated the plants; Pontefract cakes are still sold in chemists' and herbalists' shops as being good for coughs and colds, and that town is still the centre of the liquorice all-sorts confectionery

In Scotland before the war, men used to smoke liquorice sticks like cigarettes

Liquorice juice soothes stomach ulcers and pains

Mace and Nutmeg

Myristica Fragrans
France: macis/muscade
Italy: macis/noce moscata
India: tavitri/taiphal

The nutmeg is a large evergreen tree native to the
Spice Islands, and it produces both these two quite
separate spices. The ripe fruit is like an apricot and
when the flesh is removed, you find the kernel
(which contains the nutmeg) wrapped in a bright
red membrane of mace

It was not known to the ancients, but by the sixth
century A.D. both spices were being imported by
Arab traders through Constantinople

The Portuguese and later the Dutch imposed their
profitable monopolies on the trade, but their
attempts to restrict cultivation to Amboina and
Banda were thwarted by birds who ate the fresh
seeds and later vomited them on other islands.
Today, the best and sweetest nutmegs and mace
come from Grenada; those from the East Indies
have a slight aroma of turpentine

Nutmeg is sweeter and more gentle; mace, which is
sold ground or in 'blades' is more pungent. Nutmeg is used in mulled wines, stews and egg drinks;
mace may be added to baked fish and infused in
the milk of a béchamel sauce

Mustard

Brassica Alba and B. nigra
France: moutarde
Italy: senape
India: rai

Both mustards are annuals with bright yellow
flowers. The tiny seeds are the spice. The name
comes from the latin *mustum*, grape juice, with
which the Romans mixed their mustard. Through-
out the Middle Ages, it was used to enliven the
dreary winter diet; Vasco da Gama took it with
him on his first voyage to the East in 1497; and in
1720 a Mrs Clements of Durham hit on the idea
of milling the seeds and producing a mustard flour,
which found favour with George I. Two centuries
later, a Mr Colman said that he made his fortune
from the mustard that people left on their plates

Mustard baths and mustard plasters soothe aching
limbs

When the Spanish fathers established their mission
trails in California, they scattered mustard seeds to
mark the way

French mustard is made with seeds ground in
vinegar. Dry mustard has little tang when dry. It
needs about ten minutes moistened to produce its
full tangy flavour, and this will start to diminish
after an hour. For the table, therefore, fresh
mustard must be fresh

Nasturtium

Tropaeolum Minus
France: capucine
Italy: crescione

This cheerful annual, so bright a feature of many cottage gardens, takes its place as a spice because of its pungent, peppery seeds. The plant comes from the Andes, and Inca warriors are said to have chewed the seeds before battle, to kindle their fighting spirit and to daunt their enemies

The leaves bring a new taste to salads and children make sandwiches with them; the flowers can be used to prettify a fruit salad; and the unripe, green seeds can take the place of capers in salads and sauces

Paprika

Capsicum Annuum
France: paprika/poivre de Guinée
Italy: paprica

Brilliant red paprika is ground from sweet red
capsicum pods. These can vary enormously in heat
and colour; the milder variety comes from Spain,
the hotter from the Balkans. It is also grown
largely in California, and paprika has become
an important condiment in the cheaper eating
places of the United States, where it adds zest to
the staple diet of hamburgers and french fries

Paprika is good for the sight and is said to improve
night vision

Commercially, paprika is used in the manufacture
of sausages and ketchups

Paprika is a bland though gaudy spice and goes
well with cheese dishes, potatoes and eggs; the
Hungarians have taken it to their culinary bosoms
and their Goulash is its apogee

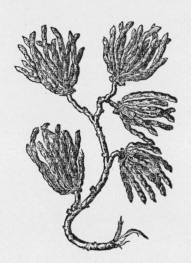

Pepper

Piper Nigrum
Peppercorns
France: poivre
Italy: pepe
India: kali mirchi

Pepper is the world's most important spice. It comes from the small round berries of a climbing evergreen shrub native to the humid jungles of Travancore and the Malabar coast of India. *Piper nigrum* is the true pepper, which the Spaniards were looking for when they encountered capsicums in Central America, to which they erroneously gave the same name. Four-fifths of the world's pepper supply now comes from Indonesia and more especially Sarawak

Sanskrit medical compendia over 3000 years old, from India, refer to pepper, and the word comes from the Sanskrit *pippali*

For many ages, pepper has formed a staple of commerce between the Orient and Europe; successively, the merchants of Alexandria, Constantinople, Venice, Genoa, Portugal, the Hanseatic ports and Holland have to a large degree owed their wealth to it. After the First Crusade, the Genoese mercenaries who seized Caesarea in 1101 A.D. were each paid two pounds of pepper as part of their loot.

Tribute has been paid in pepper. In 408, Alaric the Goth demanded 3000 pounds of pepper as part of the ransom of Rome. In the Middle Ages, pepper was so expensive and sought after that rents, taxes and dowries were paid in it; a peppercorn rental was regarded as more secure and desirable than money

When Vasco da Gama opened the sea route to the Indies round the Cape of Good Hope in 1498, the huge price of pepper was one of the inducements to the Portuguese, who then dominated the trade until the eighteenth century. Soon after, by the time London had become the world's spice exchange, increased production in both hemispheres brought down the price, and pepper was no longer the exclusive delight of the rich. Today, pepper is the only spice which you can be sure of finding in almost every household in the world

Pepper keeps well. In Sarawak, brides were dowered with pepper, which had been carefully accumulated since the day of their birth; and, during the Japanese occupation in the Second World War, hundreds of tons of pepper were buried in the jungle: when disinterred, it was found to be in perfect condition

Both black and white pepper come from clusters of berries on the vines of the pepper bush. For black pepper, these are picked while still green and unripe; they are left in piles to ferment for a few days, and then spread out in the sun to dry, until they turn black or dark brown and wrinkled. White peppercorns are the fully ripe berries, picked when they are turning red; they are bagged up and left in a stream of slow-running water for a week: this washes away the outer husk and the inner corns are dried in the sun until they turn white

Pepper is the only spice which may be used three times in one dish: first, when the food is prepared, second, when the seasoning is corrected by the cook, and thirdly, at the table, to the eater's taste

Both peppers should be ground fresh

Poppy

Papaver Somniferum
France: pavot
Italy: pepe
India: kus kus

The poppy is an annual growing in temperate climates. Its Latin name – *somniferum* – means 'sleep-bringing', and refers to the narcotic properties of the ripening poppy seed capsule, from which opium is derived. A poppy goddess was worshipped in Crete in 1400 B.C.; it was known to the ancients, and the Arabs brought it to Europe, where it was used to alleviate malaria and cholera. The opium-smoking habit hit China in the seventeenth century and ever since the poppy has been suspect. Not so its little blue or white seeds which come from the *rhoeas* variety and contain no drug

The Egyptians crushed the seeds and made therefrom an edible oil. Galen commended mixing the seeds with flour in baking bread, and the use of poppy seeds on bread spread to Europe during the Middle Ages

Poppy seeds infused in warm water provide a soothing lotion for earache and insect bites

To bring out the full nutty flavour, the seeds may be lightly toasted.

Saffron

Crocus Sativus
France: safran
Italy: safferano

Saffron is the stigma (or female organ) of a crocus,
dried. The name comes from the Arabic *za'faran*,
meaning yellow, and it has been used for thousands of years as a dye as well as a spice. Neolithic
man laid posies of saffron on the graves of his dead.
It is referred to by Homer and Hippocrates, and in
the Song of Solomon. The Greeks and Romans
spread saffron on the floors of public places, and
the indulgent Emperor Heliogabalus is said to have
bathed in saffron water – an indulgence indeed, as
it has always been the most expensive of spices

According to Hakluyt, saffron was brought to
England from Tripoli by a pilgrim, who hid
a stolen corm in the hollow of his staff. It was
especially cultivated in Essex at Saffron Walden,
the growers being called 'crokers'. In Elizabethan
England, saffron was much used in cakes and pies;
in *The Winter's Tale*, Shakespeare has the clown
plan a feast – 'I must have saffron to colour the
warden pies'

Saffron should be bought whole, and the threads
may be used thus, or crushed. Only a little should
be used: over-use will bring in a taste of medicine.

Salt

Sodium Chloride
Rock Salt
Common Salt
Sea Salt
France: sel
Italy: sale

Salt is not, of course, a spice. It is a mineral; but
its presence as a condiment on the table and as a
seasoning in cooking, together with its vital con-
tribution to a healthy diet, earn it a place here

Indispensable as the use of salt appears today, it
must have been unknown to primitive man in
many parts of the world. The *Odyssey* tells of
inlanders who knew not the sea and took no salt
with their food. In some parts of the Americas, salt
was first introduced by Europeans; and in central
Africa its use was long confined to the rich

While men were still hunters, and lived mainly
on flesh and milk, consuming their meat raw or
roasted so that its salts were not lost, they could do
without sodium chloride. But a vegetable or cereal
diet, or one where meat is boiled, needs salt, and
the honouring of it may mark the stage when man-
kind changed from a nomadic, hunting way of life
to a settled, agricultural existence. Offerings of
bread and salt were welcomed by the gods; salt

cakes were used as money and it could be that the transmogrification of Lot's wife made her more, though differently, desirable

Homer calls salt divine and Plato names it 'a substance dear to the gods', and among the ancients, as in the East today, a meal containing salt created a bond of piety and guest-friendship: hence the Arab phrase 'there is salt between us'

It is said that the oldest trading routes arose through traffic in salt; thus, one of the oldest roads in Italy is the *Via Salaria*, for carrying the produce of the salt-pans of Ostia. Herodotus's account of the Libyan caravan routes makes it clear that these were used for salt, and even today West and Central Africa, cursed with lack of salt, draw on the mines of the Sahara

Sea salt is the most easily obtainable by man, since it comes from a reservoir which covers three-quarters of the earth's surface. Salt is also mined, from deposits left behind by the oceans of primaeval times, and this is generally known as rock salt. Both may be bought in crystal form, for grinding in a wooden mill. Free-running table salt has magnesium carbonate added to stop it caking in the damp; and you can also buy common salt, for bulk purposes like salting meat or fish or a snowed-up path

There are several commercial seasonings on the market, like celery salt, garlic salt and mushroom salt. Oriental salt may be made at home, and is excellent in barbecues or with tomato juice. You will probably devise your own, ranging through your spice shelf, but here is a basic recipe –
Grind together 1 tablespoon each of celery seed and dried rosemary. Add 1 tablespoon each of paprika and ground mace, 2 tablespoons of salt and ½ a tablespoon of sugar. Mix well together and store in an airtight jar

Sesame

Sesamum Indicum
France: sesame
Italy: sesamo

An erect annual, grown in most hot countries for
its seeds and for the edible oil pressed from them.
Sesame seed mash has been found in the ruins of
Ararat; the Egyptians and the Assyrians cultivated
it; and when Ali Baba needed a password to enter
the cave of the forty thieves, he probably used
'sesame' because the ripe seeds burst from their
pod with a click like a door-lock. In 1298, Marco
Polo noted that the Persians, having no olive oil,
used sesame for the same purposes

Sesame seeds were taken to America by the slaves,
who thought the seeds were signs of good luck and
the oil a general medicine and laxative

When sesame oil is burned, the soot therefrom is
one of the main ingredients of India ink

The seeds should be lightly toasted, and can be
added to salads, potatoes, bread or rolls, and
sprinkled on cream soups. *Tahini* is a cream of
ground sesame seeds rather like peanut butter,
much used in Levantine food

Sunflower

Helianthus Annuus
France: girasol
Italy: girasole

The sunflower, a tall annual, is a native of Central
America. The Aztecs, who worshipped the sun, are
thought to have crowned their priestesses with the
flowers, often wrought in pure gold. The Spaniards
brought the seeds back to Europe and today its
handsome yellow flowers are common everywhere,
and school-children often have races to see who
can grow the highest

It is valuable in many ways. The seeds yield an excellent oil, which is used in cooking and for making
soap and candles. The flowers contain a yellow dye,
and the buds may be boiled and eaten like arti-
chokes (the Jerusalem artichoke is probably a corruption of the french for sunflower). The fibrous
stems are used in paper-making, and the plants
provide good cattle fodder

Sunflower oil is excellent with salad and, having
no smell, for frying. The seeds should be roasted;
fried until brown and salted, they are delicious
with drinks. The ground seeds are sometimes
blended to make coffee go further

Turmeric

Indian Saffron
Curcuma longa
France: Curcuma/safran des Indes
Italy: curcuma
India: haldi

A strong tropical plant of the ginger family, the harsh yellow spice comes from the underground stems or rhizomes. It has been used in the East since antiquity; Marco Polo in 1280 reported from China – 'There is also a vegetable which has all the properties of true saffron, as well the smell as the colour, and yet it is not really saffron.' In the Middle Ages, it became known in Europe as 'Indian saffron' and was used as a cheaper colouring agent

Turmeric has always been highly regarded in Asia. In Indonesia it plays a double role at weddings, rice cooked with turmeric taking the place of the Western wedding-cake while the bride and groom both dye their arms with it. In Malaysia, a turmeric ointment is rubbed on the belly of a mother after childbirth, and on the baby's umbilical cord, as an antiseptic and to ward off malignant spirits. Indian women use it as a depilatory and a cosmetic

The bright yellow colour and the pungent fragrance of turmeric add much to chutneys and pickles like piccalilli, and especially to curries, kedgerees and fish pies.

Vanilla

Vanilla Planifolia
France: vanille
Italy: vaniglia

A green-stemmed vinous plant of the orchid family;
the flavour comes from the dried, cured fruit,
usually called pods or beans. It is a native of Central
America: the Aztecs called it *Tlilxochitl*, and when
the conquistadores were in Mexico in 1520, Bernal
Diaz, one of their officers, noted that the Emperor
Montezuma was drinking *chocolatl*, ground cocoa
beans flavoured with vanilla and honey. The
Spaniards took vanilla back to Europe; in 1602,
Hugh Morgan, Queen Elizabeth's apothecary,
commended its exquisite flavour. It remained a
monopoly for almost 300 years, for only in Mexico
were found the bees and humming birds which
could pollinate the short-lived blooms. However,
in 1836 a Belgian botanist discovered a means of
hand-pollinating, and today vanilla is grown in
Java, Brazil, the West Indies, the Seychelles and
the Malagasy Republic
Although there are now synthetics, only the true
bean possesses the delicate flavour and aroma of
vanilla.

Vanilla is much used in puddings, ice creams, cakes
and custards. Commercially, it finds its way into
chocolates, soft drinks, tobaccos and scents

Grateful thanks to Mr Frank Matthews of Evans, Gray & Hood Ltd., City of London spice merchants, whose stores of spices and of reminiscences I have been allowed to raid; to Wiltshire County Libraries (Chippenham); to Mr Charles Clark for the Italian, and to Mrs Patrick Salt for the freedom of her library of cookery books.

Sources Consulted

The Art of Cookery, 'A Lady', London, 1763

The Book of Spices, Frederic Rosengarten Jr, Livingstone, New York, 1959

The Book of Perfumes, Eugene Rimmel, Chapman & Hall, London, 1865

The Complete Book of Herbs & Spices, Claire Loewenfeld and Phillipa Back, David & Charles, Newton Abbot, 1974

The Constance Spry Cookery Book, Rosemary Hume, Dent, London, 1956

The English Physitian, Nicholas Culpeper, London, 1653

The Herball, John Gerard, 1597

Herbs, Flavours & Spices, Elizabeth Mayes, Faber & Faber, London, 1963

The Roman Cookery Book by Apicius, Barbara Flower & Elizabeth Rosenbaum, Harrap, London, 1958

The Encyclopaedia Britannica, Ninth edition, A & C Black, Edinburgh, 1875

The Bible, King James' Version

The Talmud